This project is sponsored by

Kern County Children
and Families Commission

Funded by Proposition 10

OUR SOLAR SYSTEM

Mercury

BY DANA MEACHEN RAU

Content Adviser: Dr. Stanley P. Jones, Assistant Director, Washington, D.C., Operations, NASA Classroom of the Future

Science Adviser: Terrence E. Young Jr., M.Ed., M.L.S., Jefferson Parish (La.) Public Schools

Reading Adviser: Dr. Linda D. Labbo, Department of Reading Education, College of Education, The University of Georgia

COMPASS POINT BOOKS

MINNEAPOLIS, MINNESOTA

For Allison

Compass Point Books
3722 West 50th Street, #115
Minneapolis, MN 55410

Visit Compass Point Books on the Internet at *www.compasspointbooks.com*
or e-mail your request to *custserv@compasspointbooks.com*

Photographs ©: StockTrek/PhotoDisc/PictureQuest, cover, 1; NASA/JPL/Caltech, 3, 10–11, 12–13, 14–15, 17, 18–19, 19 (right), 20–21; Stephen L. Kipp, 4–5; North Wind Picture Archives, 5 (right); NOAO/AURA/NSF, 6–7; Marilyn Moseley LaMantia/Graphicstock, 8–9, 11 (right), 26–27; USGS, 16, 22–23; NASA/Johns Hopkins University Applied Physics Laboratory, 24–25.

Editors: E. Russell Primm, Emily J. Dolbear, and Karen Commons
Photo Researchers: Svetlana Zhurkina and Jo Miller
Photo Selector: Karen Commons
Designer: The Design Lab
Illustrator: Graphicstock

Library of Congress Cataloging-in-Publication Data

Rau, Dana Meachen.
   Mercury / by Dana Meachen Rau.
      p. cm. — (Our solar system)
   Includes bibliographical references and index.
   Summary: Describes the size, characteristics, and composition of the planet Mercury.
   ISBN 0-7565-0200-4 (hardcover)
   1. Mercury (Planet)—Juvenile literature. [1. Mercury (Planet)] I. Title.
   QB611 .R38 2002
   523.41—dc21   2001004417

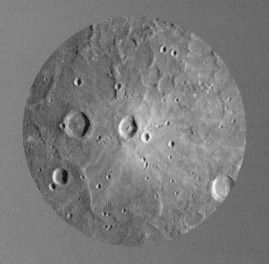

Table of Contents

Looking at Mercury from Earth

⁂ Have you ever run around a tree? Next time, pretend the tree is the Sun. Then pretend you are the planet Mercury. Run around the tree as fast as you can. At the same time, try to spin one and a half times every trip around. You would probably get very dizzy!

Sky watchers have been looking at Mercury for more than 5,000 years. The ancient Romans noticed that Mercury moves very quickly across the sky. They named Mercury

Early in the morning, you can see ▶ Mercury low in the sky.

after their god of travel, because Mercury traveled so fast.

Mercury is the closest planet to the Sun. The glare from the Sun's light makes it hard to

◀ The closest planet to the Sun is named after Mercury, the Roman god of speedy travel.

see Mercury from Earth. The best time to look for this planet is just before the Sun rises in the morning, or just after it sets at night. Mercury is very low in the sky at these times.

A large **telescope**, called the Hubble Space Telescope, circles around Earth in space today. Even the Hubble cannot look toward Mercury. The Sun's light would damage it. On Earth, most **astronomers** look at Mercury during the day. Their telescopes have special tools that block out the Sun.

◀ *The McMath-Pierce telescope at Kitt Peak National Observatory in Arizona is the largest solar telescope in the world. Scientists use this telescope to view Mercury.*

Looking at the Way Mercury Moves

✴ Mercury travels around the Sun in a path called an orbit. Mercury moves very quickly. One trip around the Sun takes eighty-eight Earth-days. Mercury only rotates, or spins, three times during two trips around the Sun. One rotation equals one day. So one day on Mercury, from sunrise to sunrise, lasts fifty-nine Earth-days!

Imagine you are standing on Mercury. You would see the Sun move strangely across the sky. As it rose in the sky, it

Mercury revolves around the Sun ▶ once every eighty-eight Earth-days. It follows an oval-shaped path.

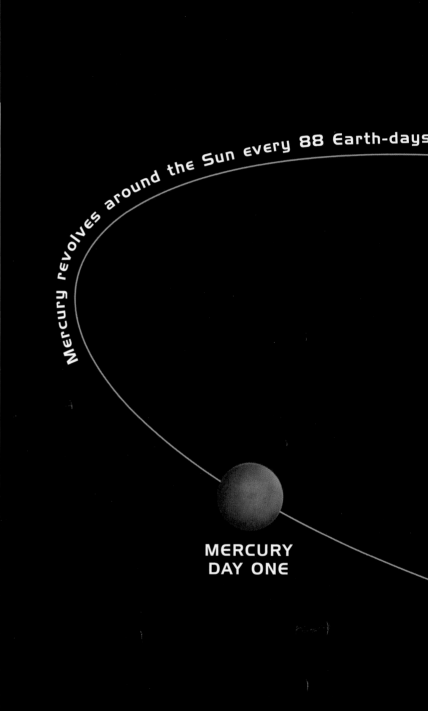

Mercury revolves around the Sun every 88 Earth-days

MERCURY DAY ONE

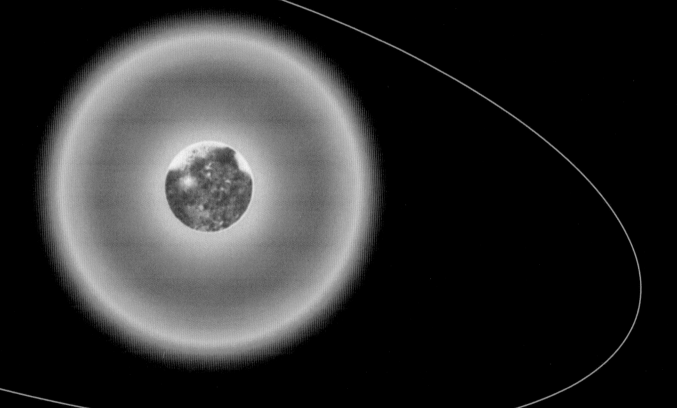

MERCURY
DAY TWO

Mercury rotates one time every 58 ⅔ Earth-days

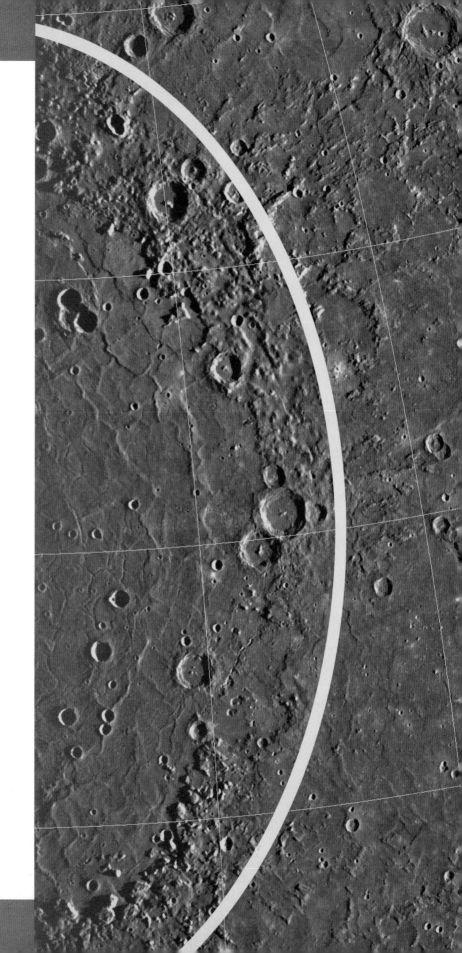

would get larger and larger. Then, when it was overhead, it would stop, go back a little way, and stop again. Then it would continue forward, growing smaller and smaller. Finally, the sun would set on the other side. This is because Mercury's orbit is elliptical, or oval-shaped. Sometimes Mercury is closer to the Sun than at other times. At its closest, it is only 29 million miles (47 million kilometers) from the Sun. At its farthest, it is 43 million miles (70 million kilometers) away.

The Caloris Basin (the half-circle on the ▶ *left side of picture) is one of the hottest places on Mercury. Its name comes from the Latin word for heat.*

The mantle and a thin crust ▶▶ *surround Mercury's huge core.*

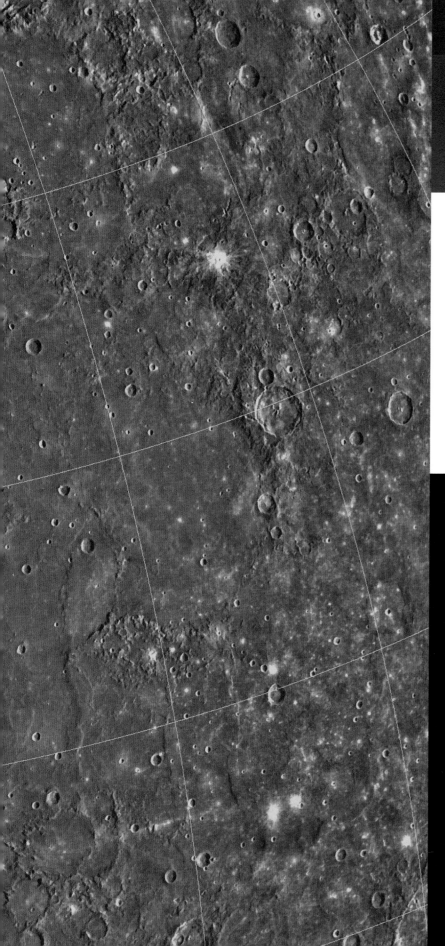

Looking Through Mercury

⚝ Mercury is called a rocky planet. That is because it is made mostly of rock and iron. The other rocky planets are Venus, Earth, and Mars.

Mercury is very heavy for

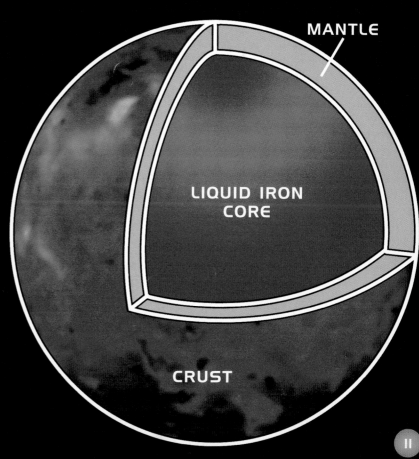

MANTLE

LIQUID IRON CORE

CRUST

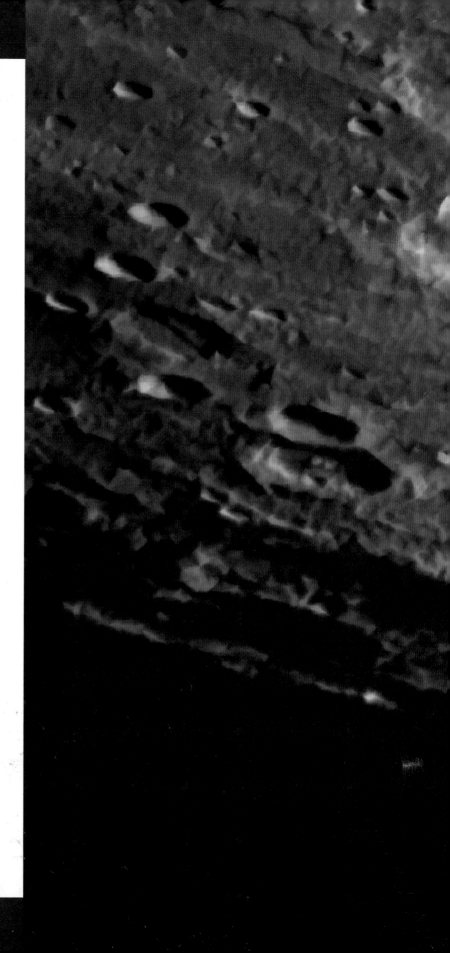

its small size. This might mean that Mercury has a large core, or center, made of solid or liquid iron. The core probably takes up about three-quarters of the whole planet. The core is covered by a thin layer of rock called the mantle. Around the mantle is the outer layer of rock, or crust, which is only 373 miles (600 kilometers) thick.

Almost every planet has an atmosphere. An atmosphere is made up of the gases around a planet. On Earth, our atmosphere makes weather, such as wind and rain. The

Some deep craters near Mercury's south ▶
pole contain ice.

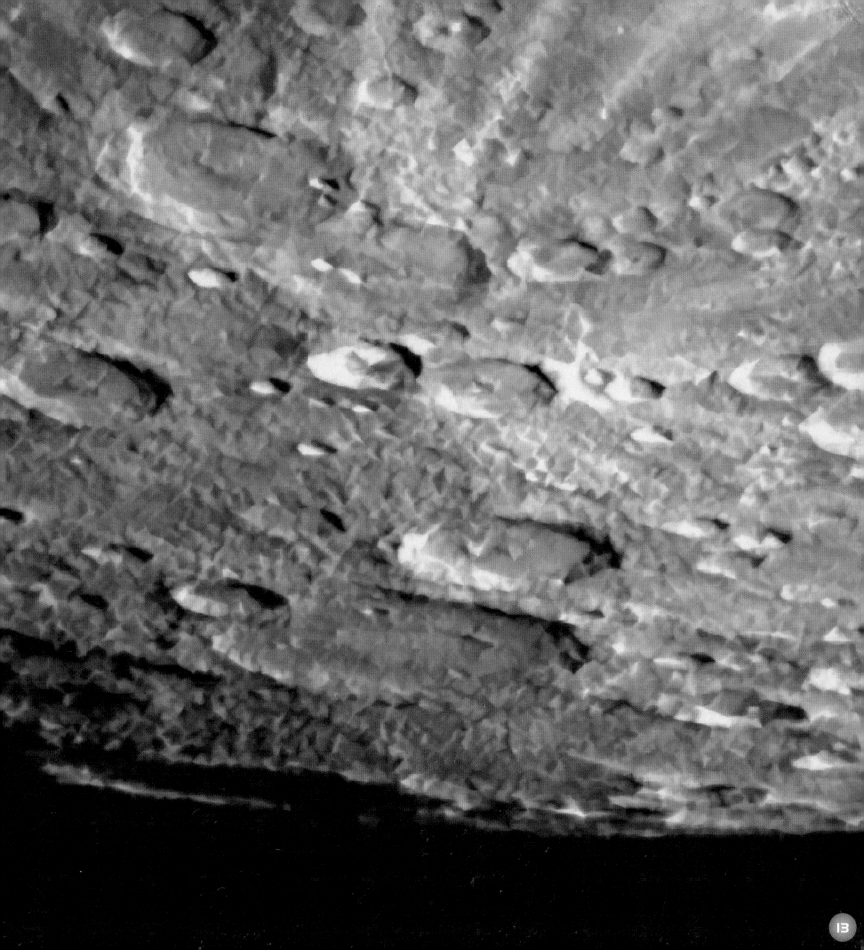

atmosphere also protects us from objects flying through space that might hit Earth. Objects, such as meteoroids, burn up in the atmosphere before they can reach the ground. But Mercury has almost no atmosphere. There is only a tiny bit of gas—hydrogen, sodium, and oxygen—around the planet. This is not enough to protect Mercury's surface from flying objects. As a result, Mercury is covered with many deep craters. In addition, Mercury has no wind or rain to erode, or break down, its bumpy surface.

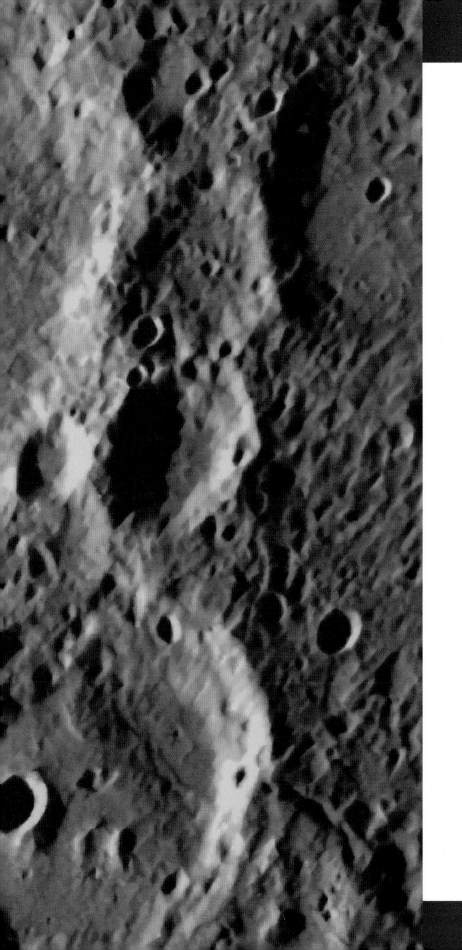

In 1991, scientists found something on Mercury that they didn't expect: water! Mercury has almost no atmosphere and is very close to the Sun. So they thought Mercury's surface would be too hot for water. But they found small amounts of ice inside some very deep craters. The craters are near the top and bottom of the planet—at its **poles** where sunlight does not reach.

◄ *Craters of all sizes cover Mercury's surface.*

Looking at Mercury's Surface

Mercury has been called the planet of "fire and ice." Some parts of Mercury are very hot and some are very cold. One side of Mercury faces the Sun, and the other side faces away from the Sun, for a very long time (fifty-nine Earth-days). So Mercury's **temperatures** change more than those of any other planet in the **solar system**. Temperatures can reach 872° Fahrenheit (467° Celsius) on the sunny side of the planet. It

Mercury's day side is hundreds of ▶
degrees warmer than its night side.

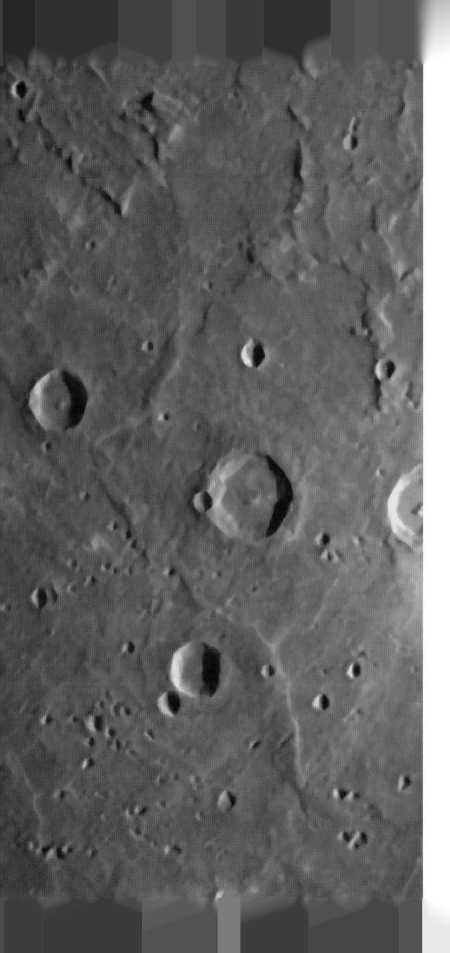

can be as cold as –300° Fahrenheit (–184° Celsius) on the dark side.

The craters covering Mercury were made billions of years ago. Scientists believe that the solar system began as a huge spinning cloud of gases and dust. Some of this material clumped together to form the planets. Meteoroids, **asteroids,** and other pieces of rock crashed into the planets. This formed craters on the planets' surfaces. This may be what happened to Mercury. The largest crater on Mercury is called the Caloris Basin. It is

◄ *Some areas of Mercury's surface are smooth and have very few craters. These smooth plains were formed by lava flows.*

800 miles (1,300 kilometers) wide and was probably created when an asteroid hit the planet.

The planet was also very hot at that time. Many volcanoes erupted and poured lava onto the surface. The lava formed Mercury's smooth plains. The planet shrank when it cooled down. This created a bumpy surface. Mercury has wrinkled ridges and huge cliffs that are hundreds of miles long and up to 2 miles (3 kilometers) high.

Astronomers have a special way of naming landforms on Mercury. They name

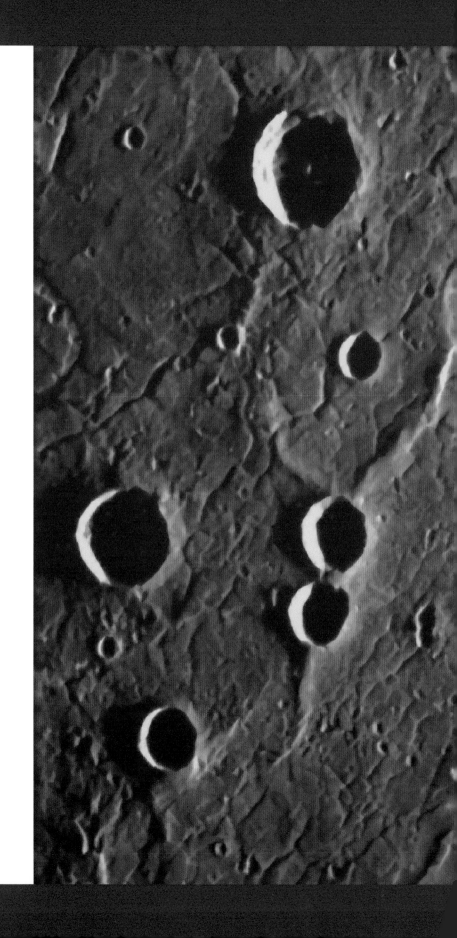

Many huge ridges cover ▶
Mercury's surface.

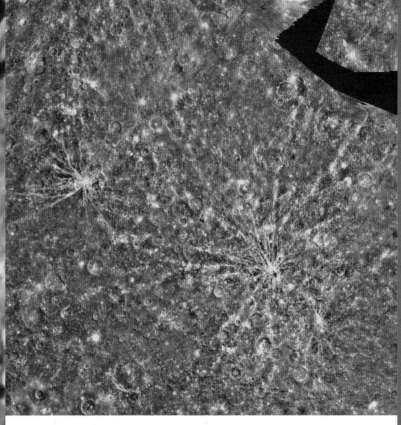

craters after artists, musicians, and writers. They name valleys after observatories—the buildings on Earth where people study space. Ridges and cliffs are named for ships that have explored Earth.

▲ *This region of craters is named after the composer Ludwig van Beethoven.*

Looking at Mercury from Space

Scientists send spacecraft into space to look at the planets more closely. One spacecraft, called *Mariner 10,* was launched into space in 1973. First, it passed Venus. It used the gravity, or pull, of Venus to help push it toward Mercury. *Mariner 10* flew by Mercury three times in 1974 and 1975.

Mariner 10 took about 10,000 pictures of Mercury. But it was only able to look at half of the planet. It ran out of

◄ *In the 1970s,* Mariner 10 *became the first spacecraft to study Mercury.*

fuel before it could finish. Still, the information and pictures it sent back to Earth have answered many questions about Mercury. They showed craters on the surface and measured the gases that make up the atmosphere.

Scientists have now lost contact with *Mariner 10*. It is probably still orbiting the Sun today. All its electronic equipment has probably been destroyed by the Sun.

*Mariner 10 took the first pictures of ▶
Mercury's surface.*

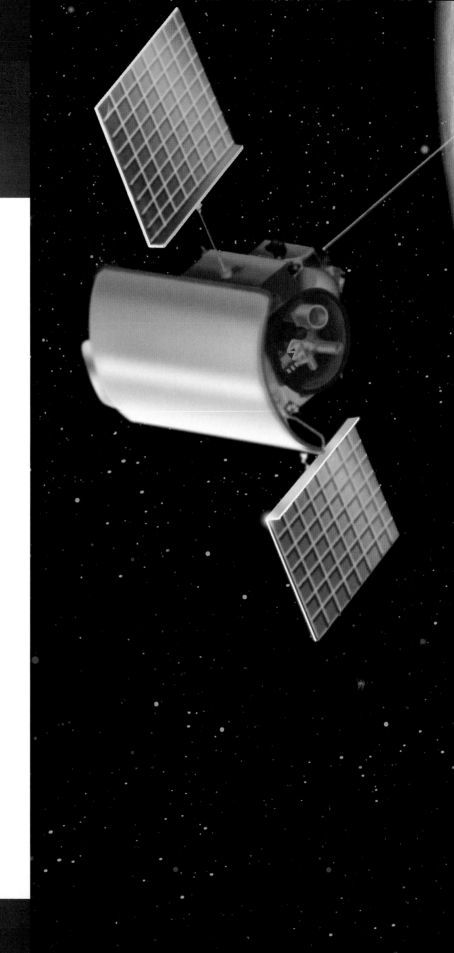

Looking to the Future

✦ *Mariner 10* could take pictures of only half of Mercury, so there is more to explore. Scientists have decided to send another spacecraft into space in 2004. It will be called *Messenger.* It will fly by Mercury twice in 2008. Then it will orbit the planet in 2009.

It is hoped *Messenger* will answer many of the questions scientists have about Mercury. They are still curious about the craters and plains on its surface. They also want to know why it is so heavy. And

they wonder about its atmosphere and water. It is hoped *Messenger* will send back information about the hidden half of the planet.

◀ *Scientists hope* Messenger *will answer many important questions about Mercury.*

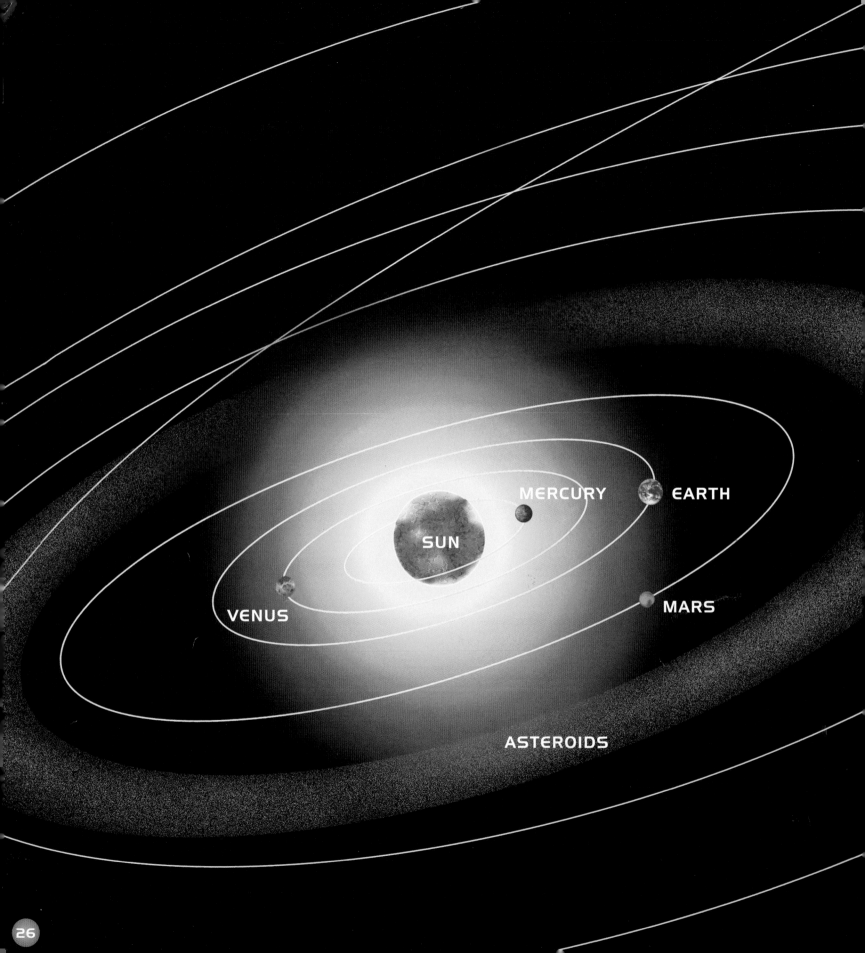

SUN

MERCURY

EARTH

VENUS

MARS

ASTEROIDS

JUPITER

URANUS

SATURN

NEPTUNE

PLUTO

Glossary

asteroids—chunks of rock that orbit the Sun especially between the orbits of Mars and Jupiter

astronomers—people who study space

craters—bowl-shaped landforms created by meteorites crashing into a planet

lava—liquid rock

meteoroids—chunks of rock in space; when one hits a planet, it is called a meteorite.

plains—flat areas of land

poles—the northernmost and southernmost points on a planet

ridges—lines of mountains

solar system—a group of objects in space including the Sun, planets, moons, asteroids, comets, and meteoroids

telescope—a tool astronomers use to make objects look closer

temperatures—measurements of how hot or cold something is

volcanoes—mountains that may erupt with hot liquid rock

A Mercury Flyby

Mercury is the second smallest planet and the closest planet to the Sun.

If you weighed 75 pounds (34 kilograms) on Earth, you would weigh 29 pounds (13 kilograms) on Mercury.

Average distance from the Sun: 36 million miles (58 million kilometers)

Distance from Earth: 48 million miles (77 million kilometers) to 138 million miles (222 million kilometers)

Diameter: 3,032 miles (4,880 kilometers)

Number of times Mercury would fit inside Earth: 18

Did You Know?

- People often think Mercury looks a lot like Earth's Moon because it is covered with so many craters.

- During the day on Mercury, temperatures are hot enough to melt some metals, such as lead.

- The Italian astronomer Galileo Galilei became the first person to see Mercury through a telescope in 1610.

- Mercury does not always look round to people on Earth. It goes through phases, much like our Moon.

- If you could visit Mercury, the Sun would look three times larger from Mercury than it does from Earth.

- Only one spacecraft has flown by Mercury, but no spacecraft has flown by Pluto.

- Mercury is the closest planet to the Sun. But there are some places on Mercury that have never seen sunlight.

Time it takes to orbit around Sun (one Mercury year): 88 Earth-days

Time it takes to rotate (one Mercury day): 58.6 Earth-days

Structure:
core (solid or liquid iron); 2,275 miles (3,660 kilometers) thick

mantle (rock) 384 miles (618 kilometers) thick

crust (rock); 373 miles (600 kilometers) thick

Surface temperature: –292° Fahrenheit (–180° Celsius) to 809° F (467° C)

Atmosphere: oxygen, sodium, hydrogen, helium, potassium

Atmospheric pressure (Earth=1.0): 10^{-15}

Moons: 0

Rings: 0

Want to Know More?

AT THE LIBRARY

Asimov, Isaac. *Nearest the Sun: The Planet Mercury*. Milwaukee: Gareth Stevens, 1995.

Margaret, Amy. *Mercury*. New York: Powerkids Press, 2001.

Ridpath, Ian. *Stars and Planets*. New York: DK Publishing, Inc., 1998.

Spangenburg, Ray and Kit Moser. *Mercury*. Danbury, Conn.: Franklin Watts, 2001.

ON THE WEB

Exploring the Planets: Mercury
http://www.nasm.edu/ceps/etp/mercury/
For more information about Mercury

The Nine Planets: Mercury
http://www.seds.org/nineplanets/nineplanets/mercury.html
For a multimedia tour of Mercury

Solar System Exploration: Missions to Mercury
http://sse.jpl.nasa.gov/missions/merc_missns/merc-m10.html
For more information about important NASA missions to Mercury

Space Kids
http://spacekids.hq.nasa.gov
NASA's space science site designed just for kids

Space.com
http://www.space.com
For the latest news about everything to do with space

Star Date Online: Mercury
http://www.stardate.org/resources/ssguide/mercury.html
For an overview of Mercury and hints on where it can be seen in the sky

Welcome to the Planets: Mercury
http://pds.jpl.nasa.gov/planets/choices/mercury1.htm
For pictures and information about Mercury and some of its most important surface features

THROUGH THE MAIL

Goddard Space Flight Center
Code 130, Public Affairs Office
Greenbelt, MD 20771
To learn more about space
exploration

Jet Propulsion Laboratory
4800 Oak Grove Drive
Pasadena, CA 91109
To learn more about the
spacecraft missions

Lunar and Planetary Institute
3600 Bay Area Boulevard
Houston, TX 77058
To learn more about Mercury and
other planets

Space Science Division
NASA Ames Research Center
Moffet Field, CA 94035
To learn more about Mercury and
solar system exploration

ON THE ROAD

**Adler Planetarium and
Astronomy Museum**
1300 S. Lake Shore Drive
Chicago, IL 60605-2403
312/922-STAR
Visit the oldest planetarium in
the Western Hemisphere

***Exploring the Planets* and
*Where Next Columbus?***
National Air and Space Museum
7th and Independence Avenue, S.W.
Washington, DC 20560
202/357-2700
Learn more about the solar system
at this museum exhibit

**Rose Center for Earth and
Space/Hayden Planetarium**
Central Park West at 79th Street
New York, NY 10024-5192
212/769-5100
Visit this new planetarium and learn
more about the planets

UCO/Lick Observatory
University of California
Santa Cruz, CA 95064
408/274-5061
See the telescope that was used to
discover the first planets outside our
solar system

Index

◄ **About the Author:** *Dana Meachen Rau loves to study space. Her office walls are covered with pictures of planets, astronauts, and spacecraft. She also likes to look up at the sky with her telescope and write poems about what she sees. Ms. Rau is the author of more than sixty books for children, including nonfiction, biographies, storybooks, and early readers. She lives in Farmington, Connecticut, with her husband, Chris, and children, Charlie and Allison.*